The Secret Garden

The Secret Garden

Shaykh Saʻd ud-Dīn Mahmūd Shabistārī

Translated by Asadullah ad-Dhaakir Yate

Zahra Publications

First published in 1982 by
Zahra Publications
Box 730, Blanco, TX 78606, USA

Republished in 1986 by
Zahra Publications
29 Ossington Street, London W2 4LZ, UK

Distributed & Republished in 2018
Publisher: Zahra Publications
www.sfhfoundation.com
www.zahrapublications.com

© Shaykh Saʿd ud-Dīn Mahmūd Shabistārī, 2018

All rights reserved. Except for brief quotations in critical articles or reviews, no part of this Book may be reproduced in any manner without prior written permission from Zahra Publications.

Copying and redistribution of this Book is strictly prohibited.
Designed and typeset in South Africa by Quintessence Publishing
Cover Design by Mizpah Marketing Concepts
Project Management by Quintessence Publishing

Set in 11 point on 13 point, Garamond
Printed and bound by Lightning Source

ISBN (Printed Version) — Paperback: 978-1-919826-87-5

Contents

Foreword 7
Introduction 11
The cause of writing this book 15
1st Question to Shabistari 19
    The Answer 19
2nd Question to Shabistari 25
    The Answer 25
    An Illustration 27
    An Illustration 28
3rd Question to Shabistari 41
    The Answer 41
4th Question to Shabistari 45
    The Answer 45
    An Illustration 48
    An Illustration 49
5th Question to Shabistari 53
    The Answer 53
6th Question to Shabistari 57
    The Answer 57
7th Question to Shabistari 61
    The Answer 61
    On the evidence of Non-existence 63

8th Question to Shabistari 65
   The Answer 65
   An Illustration 67

9th Question to Shabistari 71
   The Answer 71

10th Question to Shabistari 77
   The Answer 77
   An Illustration through Mithal 77
   An Illustration 82

11th Question to Shabistari 85
   The Answer 85
   An Illustration through Mithal 87

12th Question to Shabistari 93
   The Answer 93

13th Question to Shabistari 95
   The Answer 95
   An Illustration through Mithal 98
   An Illustration through Mithal 99
   An Illustration through Mithal 101
   An Illustration through Mithal 102

14th Question to Shabistari 105
   The Answer 105
   The Stations of the Tavern of Annihilation 108

15th Question to Shabistari 111
   The Answer 111
   Concerning Christianity 116

Foreword

"Cosmic Light is boundless and eternal. Throughout human history certain people have reflected the eternal truth of that reality, irrespective of their religious orientation or culture. Some of these sages were able to convey this in a universal light and Shaykh Sa'd ud-Dīn Mahmūd Shabistārī is one of them. Composed in 1317 CE, 'The Secret Garden' (*Gulshan-e Rāz*), continues to offer guiding insights into the realities of the Sufi path.

Shaykh Sa'd ud-Dīn Mahmūd Shabistārī was born around 1250 CE in Shabistār, near Tabrīz, in Iran during the turbulent times of the Mongol invasions. Although not much is known about his life, he wrote two collections of poetry and at least one treatise (*Haqq ul-Yaqīn*). One of two works of mystical poetry he produced, 'The Secret Garden' was composed in response to questions on profound Sufi metaphysics sent to him by a contemporary Sufi Master, Shaykh Rukn ad-Dīn Husaynī Harawī, himself a renowned Sufi master from Azerbayjan.

In this short, didactical poem of one thousand rhyming lines presented in couplets, Shabistari skillfully references the body of poetic imagery used by previous Sufi masters in their works and contributes significantly to the codification of the terms used by Sufis to signify the facets and realities of the journey to awakening to Reality. Shabistārī's penetrating answers and symbolic expositions cover critical facets of the progress of the human soul and reflect the influence of the doctrine of the 'Unity of Being' represented in the work of Ibn 'Arabī, among others. His exposition reveals the interconnectedness of reason, revelation and unveiling in the symbolic garden that offers both the thorns as well as the heady perfume of spiritual awakening. Shabistārī's answers to the critical questions posed by the nature of man in relation to the Divine can propel us along the ascending ladder of consciousness.

Long recognized as a classic of medieval philosophy and theosophy, 'The Secret Garden' was first brought to western attention in Europe in the 17th century, and continues to be appreciated as a masterpiece in the canon of Sufi literature.

In my life-long search to uncover and share the dazzling lights of Truth, I have been propelled to make available more accessible translations of certain seminal texts from the Sufi tradition. On several occasions I have had visions about Shaykh Shabistārī and others like him, including Ibn 'Arabī, Mulla Sadrā, Shaykh Rūzbehān Bāqli, and Ibn 'Atā' Allah al-Iskandarī, in which they would look at me with puzzled, smiling expressions, until at last I heard a voice telling me, 'You do not need to redo the classical works of the past, for they were for the people of that time. Truth is eternal at every point in time. Now you need to answer the questions for your time'. I hope to address these questions in that spirit in a forthcoming book.

Shaykh Fadhlalla Haeri
White River, August 2018

Introduction

In the name of the One who taught man to reflect and who lit up the lamp of his heart with the light of the spirit.

By His overflowing, both the seen and the unseen worlds were illuminated — by His abundant *fadl* the day of Adam was transformed into a garden.

His power made both the worlds appear in the blink of an eye with the command of the *kaf* and the *nun*.

When the *qaf* of His power breathed life into the pen, thousands of pictures were drawn on the empty tablet of pre-creation.

By that breath appeared the two worlds and by the same breath the spirit of Adam was manifested.

Intellect and discrimination were given to Adam so that he might recognize the source of all things.

When he saw himself as a separate individual he reflected upon his identity, asking: 'What am I?'

He made a journey from separation to gatheredness and from there returned again to the world.

He recognized the world as an illusory matter of relativity just as the number one becomes multiplied in all subsequent numbers but remains one.

The world of creation and its management came into being in one breath and at that very moment of its appearance disappeared again.

But here it is not a question of coming and disappearing since disappearance, if you reflect, only means reappearance.

All things are returning to their source — both the hidden and the manifest become one thing.

Allah, the most Sublime, who creates and destroys the two worlds with one breath, is permanent, existing beyond endless time.

In this respect the world of creation and its management are one thing — what is gathered in oneness becomes many in separation and many are gathered in oneness.

This picture of other-than-Him is from an illusion in you: this illusion is like a single spark which appears as a circle of fire when it is whirled around quickly.

Everything from the beginning to the end is pointed in the same direction and all the world's creation is moving along this single path.

The prophets are like caravan leaders, guides and masters of the travellers on this road.

Our master Muhammad, peace be upon him, in the matter of prophecy of both the first and the last became the chief from amongst them.

The One (*Ahad*) became manifest in the *mim* of Ahmad and with the completion of this cycle the first emanation became as the last.

There is a difference of only a *mim* between *Ahmad* and *Ahad*, but within that one *mim* the whole world is immersed.

He was the seal at the end of this path and in him was continued the message, 'I call to Allah'.

His heart-ravishing station is annihilation with sobriety and the beauty of his spirit's perfection is a light to the gathering of the *awliya*.

He went ahead and the hearts of all followed behind grasping his cloak for guidance, and with it sealing a pact of allegiance.

The *awliya* of this path, both before the master Muhammad and after him, have given indications of their inner experiences.

When they became aware of the parameters of the self, they described the gnostic traveller who acquires knowledge, and Allah: the source of this knowledge.

One from the ocean of gatheredness said, 'I am the

Real'. Another spoke about intimacy and distance and the progress of the boat of the separate self on the ocean of gatheredness.

One who had mastered outer knowledge of the *shari'a* gave indications from the safety of its dry land and shore.

One brought up the jewel of knowledge and became a target of the envious, another let it be and it remained protected in its shell.

Another spoke openly about the world of separation and then about the gathered whole.

One began to explain the nature of before-endless-time and the creational event.

One described the meaning of the curl, the mole and the down, and made clear the meaning of the wine, the lights, and the beautiful Beloved.

One warned about the nature of his own existence and illusions of the mind.

One sinks into idol worship and wears the Christian priest's belt.

Since each man's speech is a reflection of his station, the common people find it difficult to understand this variety of experience.

Whoever is confused about the meaning of this must seek to understand it.

The cause of writing this book

Seven hundred and seventeen years had passed after *hijrah* in the month of *Shawwal,* when a messenger with the finest courtesy and manners arrived in the service of the people of Khorasan.

There lived a man of knowledge, a spring of gnosis and a source of light with regard to his vast knowledge.

All the people of Khorasan, both the elite and the common, said he was the most knowledgeable of his age.

He had written a letter on the subject of inner knowledge and had sent it to the various masters of this science of the heart.

In it were several difficult expressions, common in the language of the gnostic masters of indication, which had been arranged as a series of questions in verse form and contained a great wealth of meaning in a few words.

When the messenger read the letter it caused astonishment in the faces of those present.

All the noble company present at the meeting one by one turned their attention towards me — a humble dervish.

One from among them, who was an experienced man of the path and had heard me talking about this inner knowledge many times, asked me to give the answers there and then so that the company present might take benefit.

I replied to him 'What need is there?' as I have several times written about this matter in my letters.

One however declared, 'We had hoped to have the answers to the questions in poetic form.'

At his insistence I began an answer to the letter in the briefest possible form.

And I immediately spoke about the whole matter without any hesitation or repetition.

I hope that the messenger will refrain from criticizing me, given his exquisite courtesy and good manners.

Everyone knows that I have never in my life intended to write true poetry.

Although I am naturally inclined to it and am capable of composing in verse, I have rarely had to read it out loud.

The cause of writing this book

Although we have written many books we have never composed poetry in *masnawi* form.

Neither prose nor verse, however, is capable of expressing the inner meaning, for this meaning is from the heart and cannot be contained in mere letters.

These inner meanings will never fit these words just as the Red Sea will never fit into a bowl.

Since I myself am in difficulty concerning the inadequacy of words, why should I increase the difficulty by using poetic language?

This explanation is not out of false modesty but is undertaken in a spirit of humility and gratitude to Allah and is an apology to the gnostics for any inadequacy in the verse.

I myself am not ashamed of the poetry since a poet such as 'Attar only appears once every hundred years.

If the inner meanings of a hundred worlds were likewise contained in my verse it would be as the tiniest whiff from 'Attar's perfume shop.

This work, however, is the fruit of experience and is not copied like knowledge overheard and stolen by the *shaytans* from the angels.

So finally I gave explicit answers to each of the questions in the letter.

The messenger accepted the reply with great respect and left by the same road he had come.

The same nobleman who had previously urged us to

answer again requested us to give a more detailed, deeper reply.

And to make clear the same inner meanings already mentioned by describing their source in knowledge and how they manifest in the outward.

'Explain more fully these meanings you talk about, demonstrate clearly how one progresses from mere outer knowledge of certainty to the very source of certainty.'

It did not seem possible for me to give an adequate answer which would truly reflect the tasting of each spiritual state.

This is impossible to describe in speech and only the one tasting the state knows the nature of the state.

But heeding the words of the Master of the *din* of Islam, I could not refuse anyone who asks about the *din*.

So in order that these secrets might become clearer I began to declare what my heart had been taught.

I described the whole subject in a short time with the help and blessing of Allah.

When my heart requested from Allah a name for the book, the answer came to my heart — 'The Secret Garden'.

As Allah Himself gave the book the name 'The Secret Garden', the inner eye of all men's hearts is illuminated by it.

1st Question to Shabistari

The first matter is that I am bewildered by my own thoughts — explain what is the process called thinking?

The Answer

You ask me to explain to you what thinking is, as you are still confused as to its meaning.

Thinking is travelling inwardly from illusory non-existence to the Real — that is leaving the separation of multiplicity for the gathered whole.

The thinkers who have written about this subject say

the following when they are explaining it:

When an image appears in the heart the first name we may give it is a recalling.

When one moves on from this by the action of thinking this is usually called interpretation or a process of learning.

The perception and ordering of these images is called thinking by the people of intellect.

A matter which is at first not understood becomes clear from the arrangement of various images which are understood.

The first proposition is as a father, the following a mother, and the conclusion issuing from them the son, or brother.

The nature of the process in question necessitates the application of the laws of logic.

And if there is no help or inspiration from Allah this process becomes a mere imitation of a set pattern.

This path is distant from our way so leave it and do without, just as Musa for a time threw away his staff.

Come into the valley of Ayman, the valley of purification and vision that the bush may in *tajalli* say to you. 'Indeed, I am Allah.'

The man of *haqiqah* who lives witnessing the Oneness of the Real sees everything first by the light of existence itself.

By his intimate knowledge of Allah his heart sees only pure light and he sees only Allah in everything.

Positive thought and correct seeing are dependent on the stripping away of the self and then help arrives with the gleams of dazzling light.

Whoever is not shown the way by Allah can never find it by use of logic.

The philosopher-thinker is basically bewildered as he sees nothing in creation but the illusory world of phenomena.

He tries to prove the Ever-Real by the transient phenomena and because of this, becomes bewildered in the essence of the Ever-Real which contains nothing of the transient.

Sometimes he progresses in understanding but then becomes paralyzed in circular thought patterns. Sometimes he becomes entangled in his chains of thought.

Since his intellect is submerged in illusory existence his very feet are enmeshed deep in the chains of cause and effect.

All things become clearly visible by their opposite but the Real has neither likeness nor opposite.

Since there is no opposite or likeness to the essence of the Real I do not know how one can know Him.

There is no likeness for the Ever-Real to be found in the passing world of forms — how is He to be known now?

How stupid is he who would look for the blazing sun in the desert by the light of a candle.

If the Sun were always in one position, its rays would

shine from only one direction.

No one would realize the beams were from the Sun — there would be no difference between the disc of the Sun and its light.

Know that the whole cosmos is visible by the rays of light from the Real — and the Real within it is hidden from sight.

As the light of the Real is constant there is no change in the appearance of things.

You imagine that the world itself is permanent, existing by its own nature.

Anyone who has excessive powers of reasoning will always encounter much confusion.

It is because of this over-reading, inquisitive reasoning that one man becomes a philosopher and another believes in incarnation.

Intellect can never bear to look at His face. Leave! And look for another inner vision that will contain Him.

As both eyes of the philosopher see double he is incapable of seeing the unity of the Real.

From this blindness comes belief that Allah is visible in bodily form in His creation and from partial blindness belief in His total separation from it.

The false belief in the movement of the spirit from one body to another at the time of death arises from the same short-sighted vision.

Such vision is like that of the blind man cut off from

seeing perfection or of the man whose path follows those who see man as essentially imperfect.

Men of book-learning who have never tasted *tawhid* are living in darkness, as if in a fog, blindly imitating the laws of outward behavior.

Men of the outward have poor eyesight, seeing nothing but the immediately obvious in the outwardly manifest.

Whatever they say about *tawhid* is nothing but reflections of their own individual way of looking.

His essence is free of and unaffected by such questions as 'how many?' 'how?' or 'why?' — may His glory be raised above whatever men say of Him.

2nd Question to Shabistari

What kind of reflection is a condition of the path — why is it sometimes necessary and sometimes wrong?

The Answer

Reflection is a condition of the path, but to think about the essence of the Real is completely wrong.

It is false to think about the essence of the Real — know that it is impossible to deduce the nature of the Real from the outwardly manifest.

The manifest signs of Allah become visible from the

hidden essence — the essence is not visible from the essence.

The whole cosmos is made visible by His light. Where does He appear manifest in the cosmos?

The light of essence is not contained in the visible world as the glory of His majesty is totally overpowering.

Abandon the intellect and stay only with the Real — the eye of the bat cannot bear the light of the Sun.

Since the light of the Real is proof of this matter what need is there for a meeting with Jibril?

Although the angels have a position close to His throne they do not have the station of 'one with Allah'.

Just as His light burns the wings of angels, so it burns the intellect from head to foot.

When an object you are looking at is very close to the eyes, perception is obscured and you cannot see it.

This darkness is the light of the essence if you only knew it — it is the water of life in a desert of darkness.

Thus darkness is only the restriction of the light of normal vision — abandon looking, since this is not the way if you desire inner vision.

What relationship has dust to the world of the unseen? Intellectual perception alone is unable to perceive the source of perception.

The darkness of separation can never be removed from the veil of illusion in the two worlds, but only Allah knows.

The darkness of separation may be seen on the face of the *faqir* in both worlds, but annihilation brings another vast darkness.

What should I say, since this matter is pure meaning?

It is a bright night within a dark day.

I have much to say concerning this kind of witnessing of the lights of the *tajalli* but to remain silent is better.

An Illustration

If you desire to see the eye of the Sun you must use a special kind of vision.

Since the eyes of man do not have the capacity for direct vision, one can see the shining sun in water.

By this means the light is reduced and you can look at it for a longer time.

The non-existence of the phenomenal world is the mirror of the Necessary — the reflection of the brilliance of the Real is visible in it.

If non-existence is placed opposite existence a reflection immediately appears in it.

Oneness becomes manifest in multiplicity just as the number one, when counted up, becomes many.

Although every number has its beginning in the number one, there is never an end to the succession of numbers.

Since non-existence is essentially pure, the hidden treasure became manifest in it.

Read the *hadith,* 'I was a hidden treasure', so you may

discover the meaning of this hidden secret.

Non-existence is the mirror, the world is the reflection, and man is as the reflected eye of the unseen Person.

You are that reflected eye and He is the light of that Seeing. The eyes of the Real see with the eye of the Seer.

The cosmos becomes the man, the man the cosmos — there is no clearer explanation than this!

An Illustration

When we look well at the root of this matter, He is the Seer, the eye and the seen.

The *Hadith qudsi* has made the meaning of this clear — the station of being 'without sight' and 'without hearing' indicates this.

Know the world is a mirror in every aspect: each atom contains a hundred blazing suns.

If you split the heart of a drop of water a hundred pure seas will appear in it.

If you look closely at every atom of dust, a thousand Adams will appear in it.

The physical structure of a fly is no different from that of an elephant — a drop of water, by its very nature, is as the Nile River.

A hundred harvests come from a single seed — the whole cosmos appears from the heart of a millet seed.

2nd Question to Shabistari

The complete cosmos is contained in the wing of a gnat and the eye of the heavens in the pupil of the eye.

In the tiny body of the heart is the station of the Lord of the two worlds.

The two worlds are gathered in it — sometimes a place for *shaytan,* sometimes Adam.

Look at the world, how everything in it is interconnected — there is an angel in *shaytan* and a *shaytan* in the angels.

Everything is interdependent as the seed and the fruit, as the *kafir* and the *mu'min*, the *mu'min* and the *kafir*.

Everything is gathered in the point of the mole — all ages and seasons, days, months and years.

The time of before-endless-time penetrates everything — the appearance of 'Isa is as the creation of Adam.

From every point in this interlinking cycle a thousand shapes are constantly forming.

Every circular point diffuses into an encompassing circumference oscillating between the center and its outer parameters.

If you were to remove one atom from its place the whole world would collapse in confusion.

Everything is in bewildering motion yet no part of it can ever slip out of its cellular reality.

The illusory world of form has imprisoned every molecule yet any separation from the whole would cause chaos.

You can say that each molecule is always between travel and rest, always between independence and dependence.

All is in movement yet always at rest; neither the beginning nor the end is ever apparent.

Everything is always aware of its own source and so is always making way for the throne of the King.

Beneath the veil of every atom the dazzling majesty of the Master's face lies hidden.

Now that you have heard these words about the nature of the world, come and say what you have seen of the world.

What do you know of the sensory and the meaning? What is the *akhirat* (far world) and what is *dunya* (near world)?

Say, what is the meaning of the *simurgh* and the Mount Kaf, what is the Garden, the *Barzakh,* and the Fire?

What is this world which is not visible, one day of which is equal to a year here?

Indeed that world is not the one you see — have you not heard Allah's oath, 'By what you do not see'?

Come and show me what the spirit world of Jabulsa are.

Reflect upon the east and the west — this world does not contain more than one of each.

Explain why Allah created the Earth 'as the seven heavens': Listen to the sultan of commentators Ibn 'Abbas and then realize it for yourself.

You are asleep and your seeing is an illusion — all you see is as *mithal*.

On the morning of the final gathering when you awake you will realize that all is illusion and idle thought.

When the illusion of double vision disappears the Earth and the heavens will become transfigured.

When the Sun of the whole cosmos displays His face the light of Venus, the Moon, and the familiar sun disappear.

If one of His rays falls on hard stone it disintegrates like wool of different colors.

Know that although you are now able to understand there is no use in knowing as you are powerless.

What can I tell you of the worlds within the heart, you, or man, with your head downcast and your feet in the mud?

The world is yourself and yet you remain incapable of realizing this — never has anyone seen a more wretched creature than you.

You are as prisoners always sitting in one position — you bind your own foot with your own helpless hand.

You sit like women in the place of misfortune, you have no shame for your state of ignorance.[1]

---

[1] "Two thousand years ago during the peak of the Roman Empire, women had practically no rights over anything in most parts of the world. A big revolution in womens rights arose with the advent of the Quran and the prophet Muhammed (*pbuh*) where the message that one's value is as good as their connection with the light of God, men or women, was revealed. Women's status was uplifted by this message, spiritually as well as materially. They were positioned as different to men, but not inferior. The expectation was that this upliftment would continue even after the death of the prophet Mohamed (*pbuh*). Shaykh Shabistārī refers in the above sections to the issue that society did not sufficiently honour this message and practice that women are equal in as far as the highest aspect of life is concerned, the *Ruh's* (soul) divine presence at heart."

The fearless warriors of the world are covered in blood and you stay with your head veiled by the rules and laws and do not step into the fight.

How do you understand the life of the weaker sex in this *din*? Do you think their ignorance is lawful for yourself?

Just because women are lacking in intellect and understanding of the *din,* do you think men should take their path?

If you are a man, come into the open and keep watch — pass by anything that obstructs you.

Do not stay day and night in the same station; do not be hindered on the path by your fellow travellers.

Go and seek the Real, like the friend of Allah, Ibrahim — turn night into day and day into night.

The stars, with the Moon and the vast sun, are in turn the senses, the imagination, and the light of the intellect.

Turn your face away from them all, oh traveller. Like Ibrahim, keep saying, 'I do not love them because they fade and set'.

Like Musa, son of 'Imran, go forward on this road, until you hear, 'truly I am Allah'.

As long as the solidity of your existence remains standing, the answer to the words 'show me' is: 'You will not see Me'.

The Real attracts you as amber attracts straw — if the solidity of your existence were not there, there would be no distance left to cover.

2nd Question to Shabistari

If the *tajalli* of Allah shine on the solidity of existence the latter disintegrates like the dust on the path of life.

In one moment of attraction the beggar becomes the king and in one instant a mountain mass is reduced to straw.

Step out on the path of the master Muhammad's *mi'raj* and delight in all the mighty signs.

Move out of the house of Umm Hani and begin the ascent: say, 'Whoever has seen me has seen the Truth'.

Leave the *kaf* of the corner of the two worlds and sit on the *qaf* at a proximity of two bows' lengths.

The Real will give you all you desire and will show you all things as they really are.

For the one whose life is in the *tajalli* of Allah, the whole cosmos is a book of the Real, the Sublime.

The *nafs* represents the vowels and the essence of man represents the letters — the ranks of creation are as the *ayats* and silences.

Every world is a special chapter in this book; one is the *surah* of the *Fatihah* and another is *Ikhlas*.

Its first sign (*ayat*) is pure intellect which penetrates all creation and that is as the *ba'* of *bismillah*.

Secondly comes the self of creation in the *ayat* of *surat an-Nur*, the Light, as it is like a lamp of exceeding brightness.

The third *ayat* in the book is the Throne of the Merciful — read well the fourth *ayat*, it is the Throne.

After this are the seven heavenly bodies, contained in

the seven *ayats* of the *surat al-Fatihah*.

Look then at the nature of the four elements, for each has its own *ayat*.

After this there are the three kingdoms of nature whose *ayats* are too numerous to count.

The last to appear was the self of man and so the Qur'an is sealed with the *surat an-Nas*.

Do not be a prisoner of structure and nature, rather withdraw from them and reflect upon the work of the Creator.

Consider the creation of the heavens that you may turn in praise of the Real through His signs.

Look for a while how the vast heaven itself encompasses the two worlds.

Why is it called the Throne of the Merciful? What connection does it have to the heart of man?

Why are these two perpetually in motion, never taking rest for a moment?

The heart is the center of the entire universe, being as a point around which the latter circles.

In the cycle of about a day and night the Throne encompasses you completely, oh *faqir*.

All the heavenly bodies turn in motion because of it — reflect well upon how they all move in one direction.

From the east to the west, like a water wheel they are always turning without food or sleep.

Each day and night this vast sphere makes a complete

2nd Question to Shabistari

circuit of the world.

By it the other planets are likewise revolving in concentric orbits.

Contrary to the orbit of the great sphere, however, each of the other eight spheres revolves in its own circuit too.

The Throne is the regulator of the signs of the zodiac so that there is no change or discrepancy in their movements.

Aries and Taurus and Gemini and Cancer are hung from it, as are Leo and Virgo.

And so too are Libra and Scorpio, Sagittarius, Capricorn, Aquarius and Pisces.

The fixed stars are 1024 in number — they all have their positions around the Footstool.

Saturn is the guardian of the seventh heaven and Jupiter has its place in the sixth.

The fifth heaven is the house of Mars, the fourth the Sun, which adorns the world.

The third is Venus, the second Mercury, and the Moon revolves within the sphere of the Earth.

Jupiter is in Capricorn an Aquarius, and Jupiter waxes and wanes in Sagittarius and Pisces.

Aries with Scorpio is placed in Mars and the Sun comes to rest in the house of Leo.

Venus makes her house in Taurus and Libra — Mercury moves into Gemini and Virgo.

The Moon recognizes a fellow creature in Cancer when the head takes the form of a knot.

The Moon travels through twenty-eight houses and then returns opposite the Sun.

Where it becomes as an old palm frond by the order of the Powerful-Precious, the Knower.

If you reflect on this, oh perfect man, you will certainly say that these words are not false.

The words of the Real are clear in this matter — if you do not see the meaning of creation you lack certainty.

Oh man of ignorance, the life of a gnat contains wisdom, so how can there not be wisdom in Leo and Mars?

If you look at the source of the matter, however, you see that the constellations are subject to the law of the Wielder of Power.

The astrologer whose *iman* is weak says that the influence of these celestial bodies is not connected to His law.

He does not see that these orbiting heavens are subject to the law and command of the Real.

You could say that these heavens are orbiting in the cycle of day and night like the potter's wheel.

By it the wisdom of the master forms another vessel from clay and water at every moment.

Everything which is in time and place comes from one Master and one workshop.

If the stars are the people of perfection why do they reveal their imperfection by setting?

Why are they all of different qualities, changing in place

2nd Question to Shabistari

and motion, and color and size?

Why are they sometimes in nadir and sometimes in zenith, sometimes in opposition and sometimes in conjunction?

Why is the heart of the heavens full of fire, what is the passion that appears in their disparate motions?

All the stars are set in motion by this, sometimes moving above the Earth, sometimes below.

The elements, water, air, fire and earth, have taken their place below the heavens.

Each is always in action in its proper place, never crossing out of its domain even a fraction.

They are four in number contrary to each other in nature and position, yet you will always see them combined in different ways.

Each is different from every other in essence and form, but they come together of necessity when He decrees.

The triple kingdom of creation appears from them — the mineral, plant and animal.

They change into essences according to the combination of the four, just as the *sufi* becomes purified of form.

All are under the command of the Master, all are subject to His mercy, remaining in their places, obedient to His will.

The minerals are reduced to lie in the dust by His power, and the plants, by His mercy, stand upright.

The sexual instinct of the animals is natural and open

in them — by it they preserve the genera, species and kind.

All confirm the law of the Lord, seeking His face night and day.

Reflect well for once on your own origin, that your original mother had a father who was also her mother.

Recognize the cosmos complete within yourself — everything which appears, appeared first in your perception.

The form of Adam appeared the last — the two worlds are dependent on his essence.

There is no other final cause besides man — everything became manifest by his own self.

The gross, solid people and the ignorant are opposite to light, but they are the manifestation of Outwardness itself.

If the back of the mirror is blackened it will reflect the face of someone from its face.

The rays of the Sun from the fourth heaven are only reflected in contact with the dust of the Earth.

You are the reflection of the One whom the angels worship — for this reason the angels prostrate before you.

Every creature that goes before you has a spirit, and from this spirit a cord is bound to you.

Thus they are all under your command — the life of each is hidden in you.

You are the core of the world, its center in every aspect knows that you yourself are the spirit of the cosmos.

Your realm is the northern quarter of the world as your heart is on the upper left side of the body.

2nd Question to Shabistari

The world of the intellect and the spirit are your wealth, the Earth and heavens are your clothing.

Consider the non-creation before creation and how it is the very source of creation — consider height, how it is the essence of depth.

For this each man possesses various organs, limbs, members and sinews.

Physicians are amazed at this; they become bewildered at the complexity of man's anatomy.

No one has set out to gain knowledge in this matter but that his attempts at explanation are insufficient.

Each organism has a function and order from the Real, each appears and returns to the Supreme Name.

All creation is sustained by that Name and is in constant praise of that Name.

Each issues from it in the beginning and each leaves by it on its return.

Although it passes from door to door in its life, it thus leaves by the same door it entered.

Thus you may know all the names, since your existence is an image reflected from these names.

Power and knowledge and will are all manifest in you, oh slave! Oh man of bliss!

You and your hearing, sight, life, and speech are not sustained by yourself but by Him.

Day and night you are trapped in thought about yourself — it is better that you leave thought about yourself.

Since the outcome of thinking is bewilderment, this discussion on thinking ends here.

3rd Question to Shabistari

What am I? Give me an explanation of 'I'. What is the meaning of travel into the self?

The Answer

Again you question me saying, 'What am I? or 'Give me news of myself so that it is clear what 'I' means.'

When absolute being is to be indicated, the word 'I' is used to describe it.

As the truth is manifest in visible creation, you indicate it by the word 'I'.

You and I are transient phenomena, manifest from the

source of existence — you and I are the patterns cast by the latticework of the lamp of existence.

Know that form and spirit is all from one light, sometimes manifested by reflection, sometimes by inner illumination.

You say the word 'I' in every explanation — by it you indicate the *ruh* of man.

Since you have made intellect your guide you do not recognize the self, because of the multiplicity of its parts.

Go, man, and know well your self — the richness of illumination cannot be compared with the barrenness of intellect.

'I' and 'you' are higher than body and spirit since the latter are both parts of myself.

The word 'I' is not limited to man in the sense that you say 'I' means the spirit only.

Travel beyond the world of creation and place — abandon the world and discover yourself in the cosmos of the self.

From the illusory shape of the *ha* of the unseen Him two eyes are formed at the time of His witnessing.

Neither the traveller nor the path remain when the *ha* of is joined to Allah.

The Real-Existent is the garden, and illusory event is the fire — I and you are the *barzakh* (interspace) between them.

When this veil is raised from before you the parameters

of religious law and practice also disappear.

All the parameters of the *shari'ah* are derived from 'you' and 'I', since they are linked to your body and spirit.

When you and I disappear from the scene, what meaning do the mosque, the synagogue, or the monastery have?

The illusory world of creation is as the dot on the *ghayn* — when the *'ayn* of your source is purified, *ghayn* becomes *'ayn*.

The path of the traveller is no more than two steps although it holds several dangers.

One step is to leave the duality of the *ha*, and the second is to abandon the arena of existence.

From this position of direct witnessing, separation and gatheredness are one, just as the number one is present in all members.

You are the gatheredness which becomes oneness itself. You are that one that becomes separation.

A man will learn this secret if he leaves behind multiplicity and makes a journey to the One.

4th Question to Shabistari

What is the nature of the traveller? Who is this wayfarer? Who can we say is the perfected man?

The Answer

Again you ask, 'Who is the traveller on the road?' it is he who is aware of his own origin.

The traveller is the one who journeys on quickly and becomes purified of his self just as fire becomes free of smoke.

Know that his journey is a voyage of discovery away from the illusory forms of creation towards the Ever-Real, leaving behind darkness and restriction.

He travels back in stages along the same path (which has led to his separation) until he becomes a perfected man.

Know how the perfected man comes into being from the time he is first born —

He appears in the form of matter and then he is made aware of his condition by addition of the *ruh*.

Then the power of movement is given to him by the Lord of power and following this he becomes a man of will by the Real.

Awareness of the outer world develops during childhood and then the whisperings of the self begin to act on him.

When all the different faculties are gathered in him, he travels from multiplicity towards the perception of the whole.

Anger and passion become manifest in him and from them come greed, miserliness and pride.

Negative qualities appear in him and he becomes worse than a wild animal, a *jinn,* or a brute.

This point is the lowest in his descent since it is directly opposite to the point of oneness.

An endless multiplicity results from his actions; he thus stands in opposition to his original gatheredness.

If he becomes caught in this trap he wanders along aimlessly, worse than an animal.

If a light arrives from the world beyond form, from this overflowing attraction, or from a certainty of knowledge within himself, then his heart becomes joined to the light of the Real and he returns along the road he has come.

He travels the path towards a certainty of *iman* through divine attraction or his own inner certainty.

He rises above the lowest pit of *jahannam* and faces the purified ones in the station of *Illiyyin*.

Then he takes on the qualities of one who turns to Allah and becomes one of the chosen sons of Adam.

He is purified of any blameworthy action — like the prophet Idris he rises to the celestial world.

When he is freed of these bad qualities he becomes spiritualized and gains an unwavering certainty.

The Power of his separate human attributes disappears in the power of the whole, and like Ibrahim, the friend of Allah, he acquires absolute trust.

His will is joined to whatever the Real desires for him, and like Musa he enters the highest door of the Garden.

He is freed from his own knowledge and like the prophet 'Isa has access to the celestial meanings.

He totally surrenders his existence to be plundered, and follows in the path of Ahmad in his *mi'raj*.

When the last point of his perfection is joined to the first of oneness there is no place for an angel nor a messenger.

An Illustration

The prophet appears as the Sun, the *wali* as the Moon facing him in the station of 'I am with Allah'.

Prophethood is clear in its perfection, his *wilayah* is manifest in it, not hidden.

Wilayah in a *wali* is concealed but it is manifest in a prophet.

The *wali* becomes intimate through submission and shares the secret of the prophet in *wilayah*.

From the *ayat* 'if you love Allah', he discovers the path to *khalwa* and that 'Allah will love you'.

In the seclusion of *khalwa* he becomes beloved and is immersed in attraction to the Real.

The *wali* is submissive to the inner meanings — the *wali* is a slave in the realm of meaning.

His project is only fulfilled when his initial separation is joined in final gatheredness.

The perfected man is he who, in the perfection of his gnosis, does the work of a slave despite being a master.

Then when he has cut through his separation, the Truth sets the crown of Khalifate on his head.

He has *baqa'* after *fana'* and so returns again from gatheredness in the Real to his initial separation in the world.

He makes the *shari'ah* his outer garment and he makes the *tariqah* his inner.

Know that *haqiqah* itself is the core of his being; his

understanding encompasses both *kufr* and *iman*.

His behavior is characterized by praiseworthy qualities — he is recognized for his knowledge, for his doing-without, and for his awareness of his true place in the Universe.

All these qualities are with him, but he is far from them hidden by the veil of *tajalli* lights.

An Illustration

The kernel of the almond is utterly spoiled if you take it from its shell unripe.

But when it is ripe it is good without the shell — if you extract the kernel you must break the husk.

If the *shari'ah* is the shell, then the kernel is the *haqiqah* and the path of knowledge lies between the two.

Error in the path means damage to the kernel — but when it is ripe it is good without the shell.

When the gnostic reaches knowledge of certainty, the kernel becomes ripe and the shell may be broken.

His being finds no place in the illusory world, so he leaves and never returns.

But if the Sun's rays fall while the kernel is still in the shell he makes another journey from the state of perfection back to the world of separation.

A tree grows from the water and earth whose branches rise up to the highest heavens.

This tree in its turn produces another seed and this seed yields a hundred by the decree of Allah, the Wielder of Power.

Like the growth of the seed into the form of the tree, a line of movement develops from the inner point of truth into the outward form.

When the traveller on the path has completed the circuit of return to separation, then his last point as man is joined to the first of the Real.

Again, he may be likened to a pair of compasses which return to the same point from which they started.

Then when he has finished his journey, the Real places the crown of khalifate on his head.

The inner movement of the traveller is not transmigration of the soul, for in truth it is manifest in the *tajalli* lights.

And indeed they ask, 'What is the end?' and the reply is: 'A return to the beginning'.

Prophethood became manifest first in Adam, and its perfection was seen in the Seal of Prophets.

Wilayah remains after the sealing of prophecy — it becomes manifest and like the point of a planet traces another orbit of the cosmos.

Its full manifestation is in the Seal of Prophets, the *awliya* may be compared to limbs of his body, for he is the whole and they are the parts.

Since he holds a perfect relationship to the master Muhammad, mercy in all creation will be made manifest by him.

He is the *amir* of the two worlds, he is the *khalif* of the sons of Adam.

You are aware of the breaking dawn, the sunrise and the zenith because the light of the Sun is absent from the night.

From the circling of the orbiting planets you are able to see the Sun's decline, in the time between mid-afternoon, and the sunset.

The light of the Prophet is as a vast sun, sometimes shining in Musa, sometimes in Adam.

If you read the history of the world, you will know clearly the different degrees of the prophets.

Every moment shadows are cast by the Sun — each is a *wali* and a degree in the *mi'raj* of the *din*.

The age of the master Muhammad is the time of the meridian; he is purified of all shadows and darkness.

He stands upright on the equator and casts no shadows before or behind, to the right or the left.

He stands on the path of Truth and is firm in Allah's command to him: 'Be established'.

He has no shadow, for that implies darkness; how bright is the light of Allah, a shadow of divinity.

His *qiblah* is between the east and the west and so drowned in a flood of light.

When *shaytan* becomes muslim at his hand he will be a mere shadow hidden beneath his feet.

All degrees of prophethood and *wilayah* are beneath his

foot and the existence of the men of perfection on Earth is from his shadow.

The shadow of *wilayah* has spread from his light, the east of prophethood is balanced by the west of *wilayah*.

From each shadow which appeared at the beginning, another corresponding one appears at the end.

Thus each *wali* or gnostic has his reflection in a corresponding prophet from the family of the prophets.

Since a prophet is perfect in his prophethood, he is of necessity more excellent than any *wali*.

Wilayah will be made fully manifest in the seal of *walis*, the Imam Mahdi, and so with the first point in Muhammad it is perfected in the last.

By him the world is filled with peace and *iman* and by him both the mineral and animal kingdom receive life.

Not a single *kafir* will remain in the world, true justice will become openly established.

He will reach the Real by the secret of *tawhid*, and the face of the necessary will be visible in him.

5th Question to Shabistari

Who is it who discovers the secret of *tawhid*? Who is the man of knowledge who becomes a gnostic?

The Answer

The man who reaches awareness of the secret of the Oneness is he who does not stop on the various stages of the path.

For the heart of the gnostic, his knowledge is his very witnessing.

He does not recognize other than this true existence and he gambles clean away any existence other than this.

Your whole life is thorns and weeds — throw it all

completely away from yourself.

Go and sweep out the house of your heart — prepare a place for the Beloved.

When you leave, He comes in and shows His majesty to your 'you', purified of yourself.

A man becomes beloved by his extra acts of service, and he sweeps out the house of his heart by denying entry to other-than-Him.

By this he gains the station of Mahmud and indicates this hearing and vision to be no longer his own.

For as long as his own existence remains with him there is a defect, and the knowledge of the gnostic is not experienced from the source.

Light will not come into your heart until you have removed all obstacles from yourself.

As there are four obstacles in this world, there are four kinds of purification which remove them.

The first is purification from physical impurity, and the second from rebellious behavior and the whisperings of *shaytan*.

The third is purification from bad behavior which lowers man to the state of animals.

The fourth is purification of one's secret from otherness, and this marks the end of the inward journey.

Whoever reaches this stage of purification is without doubt fit to talk intimately with Allah.

How can your prayer ever be true prayer until you have

completely gambled yourself away?

Your prayer only becomes a coolness for the eyes when your essence is purified of any stain of otherness.

Then there remains no distinction between the gnostic-knower and Allah-the-known — they become one.

6th Question to Shabistari

If the knower and known are one pure essence, what use are the aspirations of this handful of dust?

The Answer

Do not be ungrateful for the gifts of the Real — you may recognize the Real by the light of the Real.

You must find out for yourself that beside Him knower and known do not exist, yet the dust may draw heat from the Sun.

It is not strange that the atoms of dust yearn for the heat and light of the Sun.

Remember your natural state in your station before creation so that you may know again the source of all true reflection.

To whom did Allah say, 'Am I not your Lord?' Who was it after all who immediately answered, 'Yes'?

On the day he fashioned the clay He wrote the nature of each man's *iman* on his heart.

If you read what is written without delay you will know everything you want.

Last night you bound yourself in a transaction of slavery, but through ignorance you have now forgotten it.

Therefore the word of the Truth was revealed to remind you of this first acceptance of the life transaction.

If you could see the Real at the beginning then you must be able to see Him again in this world.

See His attributes today in this world so that you may recognize His essence tomorrow.

If you cannot do this however, do not be destroyed by disappointment — go and listen to the *ayat*, 'You cannot give guidance to yourself' from the Qur'an.

A man blind from birth cannot believe in the existence of color, even if you demonstrate with arguments and proofs for a hundred years.

White and red and blue and yellow and green are all nothing but black to him.

Reflect upon the sorry state of one born blind at birth — how can he ever gain his sight back by the oculist's eye?

Reason, as regards its perception of the higher states of witnessing, is as a man born blind who cannot see the world.

Man has a means to discover those hidden secrets which lie beyond intellect.

Just as fire appears when flint and steel contact each other, so Allah has placed this faculty in man's spirit and body.

Thus by the combination of the inner and the outer the secret becomes manifest. Now you have heard this, go and purify yourself.

Whenever the flint and the iron meet, the two worlds are illuminated by the light which is emitted.

Your self is a copy of the divine image; seek in yourself everything you wish to know.

7th Question to Shabistari

What is the point of the words, 'I am the Real'? What do you mean by saying he was a fake?

The Answer

Within the words, 'I am the Real' lies the total discovery of the secrets — who except the Real himself can say 'I am the Real'?

You should understand that, like Mansur, all the atoms of the world are drunken with wine.

They are constantly repeating *'Subhan Allah'* and *'La ilaha illa Allah'*, and are all sustained by their *dhikr* of Him.

The Secret Garden

If you wish to understand this clearly, read the Qur'anic *ayat*, 'everything is in a state of praise'.

When you have carded the self as cotton, you, like the wool-carder Hallaj, will cry out: 'I am the Real'.

Take the cotton of illusion from your ears and listen to the call of the One, the Wielder of Power.

The call from the Real is constantly coming — why then are you waiting for the final day?

Come, like Musa, into the valley of Ayman — the bush will say to you: 'Indeed, I am Allah'.

If it is permitted for the bush to say, 'I am the Real', why then is it not permitted from the mouth of an excellent man?

Every man whose heart is free from doubt knows with the eye of certainty that there is no existence but the One.

To say 'I am', befits only the Real, for He is the unseen, the Absent, but He also encompasses the illusion of the phenomena.

His Excellency, the Real, His majesty the Truth is not two persons — 'I' and 'we' and 'you' cannot exist along with Him.

I and we, you and he are all one thing, for in oneness there is no distinction between personalities.

Every man, stripped of the self, is empty of self and the cry 'I am the Real' echoes within him.

By His face, the *Baqi* (the Ever-Continuing), otherness is destroyed, and travelling, travel, and the traveller all become one.

The arrival at oneness and union are impossible, for duality in unity is utterly false.

What we call arrival at oneness or unity only exists by virtue of the notion of otherness — realization of His Oneness is achieved through inner travel.

It is phenomenal existence that is separate from true existence — the Truth can never become the slave nor the slave, Allah.

Existence, creation and multiplicity of forms are mere appearance — not everything that seems to be really is.

On the evidence of Non-existence

Place a mirror opposite yourself, look into it and see that other person.

Look once again to see what this reflection is — it is neither the self nor the mirror; what then is that reflection?

How can non-existence and existence be joined? — after all, both light and darkness cannot exist together.

Like the past, the months or years of the future have no reality — what is there but this single point of the present?

There is but one imaginary droplet in a state of flow — you have given it the name of a running river.

There is no one else but myself in this desert of a world — tell me what are these voices and echoes of multiplicity.

Phenomenal events are transient, but the essence is compounded of them. Say, how does it exist, how is it and where is this essence?

Bodies are composed of length, breadth and depth — they exist, in that they have become manifest from non-existence.

This is the origin of the stuff of all the worlds — now you know this, have trust in Allah and stand firm.

There is no other existence than the Real — say, 'He is the Real' and if you wish, 'I am the Real'.

Distinguish the show of illusion from the existence of the Real — do not be a stranger, but become acquainted with the Real.

8th Question to Shabistari

Why do they say a man has arrived? What is the path, and the travelling, and how is arrival?

The Answer

Union with the Real is by separation from His creation, and by being a stranger to yourself so that you become acquainted with Him.

As the contingent-phenomenal is always swept away by other phenomena, nothing remains except the necessary absolute.

The existence of the two worlds is an illusion which

disappears at the moment of the continued existence in Allah.

The one who achieves union is not of creation — the speech of the perfected man affirms this too.

How can non-existence find a way to this door? What connection has the dust to the Lord of the Lords?

How can non-existence be united with the Real? How can there be travelling and a journey from it?

You are non-existent and non-existence is unmoving — how then can the non-existence of phenomena move to the Necessarily-Existent?

If your spirit were to become aware of this inner meaning you would immediately say, '*Astaghfirullah!*' (Allah cover me).

Essence without external qualities is not tangible, and what are these external qualities? They hardly last a moment.

The philosophers who have written about this natural science describe it in terms of length, breadth, and depth.

What is matter but absolute non-existence in which form becomes perceptible?

Since form without matter is not possible, matter without form is nothing but non-existence.

All the bodies of the world consist of these two non-existences and nothing is known about them but their non-existence.

Reflect upon their nature — in themselves they have neither existence nor non-existence.

Look at the world of transience in relation to the Truth — in itself it is deficient without real existence.

The Ever-Present in its own perfection pervades everything — visual phenomena are just imaginary phenomena relative to it.

Phenomenal things have no real existence — although there are many numbers they are all multiplications of the number one.

The cosmos is meanings in passing images — the whole affair is nothing but a manifestation of desires, or a theater-show.

An Illustration

The mist rises from the sea and by the command of the Real falls as rain onto the desert.

The rays of the Sun from the fourth heaven fall down and the water and dust become mixed together.

Once again the heat moves upwards and the same sea water mingles with it.

When earth and air are joined to the rays of the Sun a fresh green plant emerges.

By transformation this food becomes the animal which is eaten by man and thus transformed yet again.

In turn a sperm is produced which passes through different forms and from it man is born yet again.

When the light of the eloquent self enters the body a subtle being illumined with gnosis appears.

Thus child becomes youth, then man and old man, with gnosis and knowledges, intellect and the ability to reflect with care.

Then the time fixed by the Pure, the Ever-Present, arrives and the pure spirit returns to original purity and the clay of man mingles with the Earth.

All the separate parts of the world are as plants which themselves are single drops in the ocean of life.

When the time is up for them their end becomes their beginning once again.

Each of them returns to the central point of origin — they follow of necessity a natural principle which tends back to the center.

Oneness is like an ocean — though full of the blood of dying forms, from it rise a thousand wild waves.

Reflect upon a drop of water from the ocean, how it possesses various forms and names.

Vapor, cloud, rain, dew and clay become in turn plant, animal and the perfected man.

In fact they were all one drop of water at the beginning — all these things were formed from that.

The cosmos is composed of the intellect, the self the heavens and the planets — recognize that they are all as that drop of water in the beginning and the end.

When the appointed time comes to the heavens and the

stars. Their existence disappears into non-existence. When the wave of His power strikes, the cosmos is destroyed and then the Qur'anic *ayat*, 'It did not exist yesterday' is fulfilled.

In a moment illusion vanishes and no one remains in the world but the Real.

At that moment you achieve proximity, and stripped of yourself, you are united with your Beloved.

Arrival here means the removal of illusion, for when other-than-Him disappears there is arrival.

Do not say that the world of phenomena has passed beyond its limits — the truth is that neither the phenomenal becomes the Ever-Existent, nor the Ever-Existent the phenomenal.

No one who has reached the world of meanings claims that it was achieved by a changing of the truth.

Thousands of forms appear before man, the master — go and reflect upon your beginning and your end.

We will now explain point by point the argument concerning the part and the whole, both the manifest and the hidden aspect.

9th Question to Shabistari

What is the meaning of the union of the transient-phenomenal and the Ever-Present — what is near and far, more or less?

The Answer

Listen to what I have to say directly — what is meant by nearness is that you become far from yourself.

When true creation became manifest in the non-existence or pre-creation, then the relative qualities of near and far and more or less also appeared.

The man on whom light shines is near — anyone far

from real-existence is as a distant non-existence.

If He gives you a light from Himself, he frees you of your own existence.

What do you gain from this existence which is non-existence? Sometimes it makes you fear, sometimes it gives you hope.

A man does not fear anyone he knows — it is only the child who is afraid of his own shadow.

Fear does not remain when you begin to move — the racehorse needs no spurring on.

What fear can you have of the fire of *jahannam* when your body and spirit have been purified of existence?

If pure gold is heated in fire, what is there to burn? It contains no impurities.

There is nothing in front of you except yourself — reflect well on your own illusory existence.

If you become caught up in yourself, then the world will become your veil.

Your 'youness' is the lowest point in the cycle of existence. This youness is the point directly opposite unity.

You have taken on a particular form because of the visible, solid nature of the world — because of this, you say like *shaytan*, 'Who is there similar to me?

Because of this you say, 'I myself have free will — my body is the riding-beast and my spirit is the rider.

The reins of the body are in the hand of the spirit and so I have complete control over it.'

Do you not realize that this is the way of the fire worshippers? All this worthless deception comes from this illusory existence.

Oh ignorant man, what kind of free will is this if the very essence of a person is a non-reality?

Since your existence is complete non-existence, can you say where this free will of yours comes from?

A person's true existence is not from himself, and so in its essence can be neither good nor bad.

Whom have you seen in the whole world who has ever found happiness without pain?

Who, after all, has ever gained everything he had hoped for and remained in a state of perfection?

Spiritual stations continue in him, but the men of the stations are subject to the command of the Real — Allah holds sway over all creation.

Recognize the effect of the Real in every place — do not place a foot beyond your own limits.

Look at your own state to discover the nature of His decree and from it recognize the people who accept His decree.

The Prophet said that any men whose way was other than predestination were as fire-worshippers.

Just as the fire-worshippers talk of Yasdan and Ahraman, so these stupid fools talk about 'I' and 'me'.

Attributing actions to us is imaginary — in the world of realities the meaning of such attribution is just empty desire and play.

You did not exist when your actions were created — you were appointed for a specific purpose.

By His knowledge and power independent of any cause, He exercises complete control over the whole affair.

A specific work was predestined for every man even before his body and spirit were created.

Shaytan was obedient for several thousand years. But then was made to wear the yoke of Allah's curse.

Another however saw light and clarity after an act of disobedience — when he turned to Allah he saw the light of one who had been chosen.

Even stranger was that Adam, who disobeyed Allah's command, should receive mercy and forgiveness by the gentleness of the Real.

Shaytan was cursed because of the heedlessness of Adam. How little you notice the nature of your own actions.

The mighty King does not care — He is above all comparison that imagination conjures up.

What happened in the time beyond endless time, oh foolish man, that this man should become Muhammad and that man Abu Jahl?

Anyone who asks how and why in connection with Allah speaks without courtesy, like a *mushrik*, about his Lord.

It is permissible for Him to ask how and why, but it is not good for the slave to make objections.

His divinity comes from His being greater than everything else — to attribute cause to God's action is not fitting.

Gentleness and power are qualities of the divine — slavery however consists of poverty and obligation.

The nobility of man lies in this compulsion and not in having a right of choice in his actions.

Nothing in the course of his life is ever from himself, yet Allah asks him concerning his good and bad actions.

Man has no choice but is subject to Allah's power — how bereft is man, a man of choice but obliged to do everything predestined for him!

This is not oppression but rather pure knowledge and justice — it is not tyranny but rather mercy and generosity.

For this reason he has imposed the *shari'ah* on you and has made it known to you by the very make-up of yourself.

When you realize that the Real is responsible and you are totally incapable, then you may immediately leave the management of affairs.

You will be freed from yourself in Allah who encompasses all, and you will become rich by the Real, oh *faqir*.

Go, spirit of your father, and yield yourself to Allah's will, submit to what He has written for you.

10th Question to Shabistari

What is the sea whose coast is its speech and what is the pearl which is taken from its depths?

An Answer

Existence is a sea and speech the coast, the shells are the letters and the pearls knowledge of the heart.

It throws up a thousand magnificent pearls with every wave in the form of commentaries, texts and oral tradition.

Every instant a thousand waves rise out of it yet it never becomes less even by a single drop.

The existence of gnosis from that sea is in the depths

— the coverings of the sea's pearls are the sounds and the letters.

Since these are meanings revealed in this matter, it is necessary to make them clear by using a mithal.

An Illustration through Mithal

I have heard that in the month of Naysan, the shells come up from the depths of the sea of 'Uman'.

They rise upwards from the lowest depths of the sea and rest on the surface with their mouths open.

Vapor evaporates upwards from the sea and falls as rain by the command of the Real, the Sublime.

Several raindrops fall into each shell's mouth — each mouth then tightly shuts.

The shell descends into the sea's depths with a full heart and each drop of rain becomes a pearl.

The diver then goes down to the bottom of the sea and brings up the gleaming pearls from the shells.

Your body is the coast and the sea is existence. The vapor is divine outpourings of mercy and the rain is gnosis of the names.

Intellect is the diver in this vast sea — it carries a hundred pearls in its diving bag.

Knowledge is as a container — the shells of knowledge of the heart are the sounds and letters.

The breath of the self moves like a flash of lightning and brings the letters and words to the listener.

Break open the shell and bring out the magnificent pearl — throw away the shell and seize the sweet kernel.

Vocabulary and etymology, syntax and word-points are merely the outer clothing of words.

Anyone who devotes his life to the study of these has wasted his precious life on trivia.

Only the dry husk of the nut falls into his hand — he will never find the kernel unless he breaks the husk.

Yet the kernel without the husk remains unripe — and from knowledge of the outer, the knowledge of the *din* of Islam becomes sweet.

Strive for knowledge of the *din* with your heart and spirit — listen to my advice, oh dear brother!

The man of knowledge is raised up in the two worlds and even if he were unworthy of them, he is made more worthy.

An action which comes from the secret of one's spiritual states is much better than an action based on a knowledge one has heard, yet not experienced.

A purely physical action from man's water and clay is not true knowledge, for this is a matter of the heart.

Look at what a difference there is between the body and the spirit — you can take one to be the west and one the east.

Realize from this how actions proceed from different spiritual states and what the relationship is between informative and experiential knowledge.

Anything which loves the world is not knowledge — this knowledge has an outer form but contains no meaning.

Knowledge can never be joined with a desire for the world — if you want the angel, then throw the dog out from yourself.

Knowledge of the *din* comes from an angel-like character and this does not enter a heart which has a dog's nature.

This, after all, is what the *hadith* of Mustafa says: 'Listen well for, in truth, this is how it is'.

Moreover if any image is contained in a house the angels will never enter it.

Go and clean the face of the tablets of your heart until an angel makes his home with you.

Learn the knowledge of friendship with him and watch over your portion to come in the next world.

Read the book of truths in yourself and on the horizon — adorn yourself with the principles of all good behavior.

The principles of good behavior are justice, and then wisdom, balanced temperament and courage.

The true man of wisdom is the one whose speech and action take on the qualities of these four.

His heart and spirit are aware of wisdom, yet he is neither cunning nor a fool.

His purity of temperament protects him from his own desires — all wrong action is extinguished and disappears from him.

He is courageous and free of meanness and pride — realize that he is purified of cowardliness and carelessness.

As justice has become the cloak covering his inner core, injustice is not part of him and so all his behavior is good.

Good morals come from taking the middle way and avoiding being excessively restrictive or over-extravagant.

The middle way is the straight path of Islam which is bounded on both sides by the deep abyss of *jahannam*.

It is as fine as a hair or a sword blade — there is no room to turn around or even stand still on it.

Since justice has only one opposite quality, the opposite qualities make seven in number.

A secret is hidden beneath each one and for this reason there are also seven gates to the Fire.

Just as the Fire is always prepared for injustice, so the Garden is always the place for justice.

Light and mercy are the reward of justice, and curses and darkness are what to expect from injustice. Goodness becomes manifest in equity, and balance in the body is the height of perfection.

As a compound comes to be like one single substance, it is different from its individual components in its nature and qualities.

It becomes like a basic essence — between itself and this similar basic essence a bond is formed.

It is not the bond which exists between the compound and its parts, for the *ruh* is free from the qualities of the body.

When water and clay become purified, then immediately the *ruh* is added to them by the Real.

When the main elements come into balance, then the rays of the spirit world fall on them.

The light beams from the spirit shining on the body in equilibrium are like the rays of the Sun shining on the Earth.

An Illustration

Although the Sun is in the fourth sphere, its rays are the light which governs the Earth.

The natural elements do not exist in the Sun — the stars are neither hot nor dry, nor cold nor wet.

The elements are only cold and hot, white, red, green pink or yellow because of the Sun.

His Command is effected like that of a just king — it cannot be said to be an integral part of the elements nor completely free of them.

Since all the elements are set up in balance and harmony, the self falls in love with their beauty.

A marriage of meaning occurs according to the *din*, and the world is given as a dowry to the self which fills the cosmos.

As a result of this marriage, eloquence, gnosis, language,

morals and beauty appear.

The radiance of the world without forms comes in like a drunken rogue.

It raises its flag in the city of beauty and completely disrupts the order of the world.

Sometimes it rides astride the horse of beauty and sometimes it brandishes the sharp sword of language.

When this manifests in man it is said to be radiance, and when in speech, eloquence.

The *wali*, the king, the dervish and the rich are all subject to its command.

What is this beauty and goodness in a face? Say what it is, for it is something other than physical beauty.

This heart-ravishing beauty can come only from the Real, for the man of divine illumination is not other than, nor a partner to, Him.

How is it that lust steals man's heart and sometimes the Real manifests from the false and the impermanent?

Recognize the working of the Real in every place — do not set a foot beyond the boundary of your own self.

To realize the Real in the robes of the Real is the only true *din*, and the Real which appears in the illusory non-real is the work of *shaytan*.

11th Question to Shabistari

What is the part which is bigger than the whole?
What is the path which leads to that part?

The Answer

The existence of that part which is bigger than the whole is gathered existence that is the reflected universe.

Gathered existence appears in manifold forms in the outward and is only unified in the inner.

All-encompassing existence became manifest in plurality of form and so its unity is a part (of the rest) in movement.

The whole has many forms when seen from its outer aspect, yet it is smaller in quantity than its own part.

In fact phenomenal existence has no reality, for the Real has control over it.

The whole has no existence in the Real as it became contingent-phenomenal within the Real.

The existence of the whole is unified-plurality, the plurality manifesting in many outer phenomena.

Existence, which is gatheredness, became transient forms and these passing forms are by their very nature returning to non-existence.

As each part of the whole becomes annihilated, the whole is annihilated with the contingent-possible at the same moment.

The cosmos is this whole which at every blink of the eye is returning to non-existence and does not last a moment.

Then the cosmos appears again — the Earth and heavens are recreated every instant.

At every second the young and old advance in age — every moment is new, yet instantly old.

There is a gathering together and a dispersal contained in every breath.

Nothing remains for more than a second — in the very moment a thing dies it is born again.

This is not the final day of calamity, however — now is the time for action and that is the day when the debts are settled.

There is a great difference between this and that. Do no trap yourself in ignorance.

Look clearly into the explanation of the meanings — examine the hour and the day, month and year.

All speech and actions are stored up and will be made manifest on the day of gathering.

There the innermost core of men's hearts will be made visible — read the *ayat*, 'all the secrets will be revealed'.

An illustration through Metaphor

If you wish to understand this meaning, reflect upon how existence is both death and life.

Everything in the cosmos terrestrial and celestial, has an example which is visible in your body and spirit.

The cosmos, like you, is a specific person — you are as a spirit to it and it is your body.

Man dies in three different ways. The first death occurs in every breath because of his nature.

The second of these is the death of choice; the third is the death which is inevitable for him.

Since death and life are opposites, his life is of three kinds and in three degrees.

The cosmos has no death by choice, as you alone of all creation possess this.

Yet at any moment the world is in change, and its latest

form becomes like its first.

Whatever appears on the day of gathering will be manifest in you at your moment of death.

Your body is like the Earth and your head is like the heaven — your senses the stars, and the Sun your spirit.

Your bones are hard like the mountains — your hair is as the plants and your limbs as trees.

At the time of death your body will tremble with regret like the Earth on the final day.

Your brain will become confused and your spirit darkened — your senses will become dim like the stars.

Your pores will run with sweat like rivers, and you will drown completely in it.

At the moment of your death, oh bereft man, your bones will become as soft as dyed wool.

Your legs will be twisted together — every couple will be separated from each other.

When the spirit has become totally separated from the body, your land will become an empty plain.

The whole world will be in a similar condition and this you will see in yourself in that moment.

Going-on after death is with the Real, the rest is in annihilation — all this is explained in the opening *surah*.

It explains the meaning of 'all which exists there is in annihilation' and also makes clear the *ayat*, 'indeed He is on a new creation'.

The creation and destruction of the two worlds are like

the creation and raising of the self of the sons of Adam.

The creation is constantly becoming a new creation even though the length of its life seems long.

The outpouring and bounty of the Real, the Sublime, is being constantly radiated through His working in creation.

From one aspect there is creation and perfection and from another there is constant change and annihilation.

When, however, the form of this world has passed away, all will continue in the next world.

Thus everything which you see contains, of necessity, two worlds — that of form and meaning.

Connection with the first means total separation and with the other a life continuing in Allah.

Going-on with Him is a name for true existence, but its place is in flow, never at rest.

As the outer-manifest forms depend on the One who manifests, this world is the very reflection of the next world.

Whatever is only potential in this world will be realized in that world to come.

Every action which at first proceeds from you is mastered by you when you repeat it several times.

Every time you do it, whether for gain or loss, traces are stored up in the self.

Through habit the states of the heart become normal for you — it is with the passing of time that fruits become pleasantly flavored.

It is through habit that man learns the various trades

and learns to put his thoughts in order.

All man's actions and sayings are as if stored up and recorded — they will become manifest on the day of gathering.

When you are stripped of the clothing of the body, both good and bad qualities will become clear.

It will be your body, but without impurity, so that forms will be reflected in it as in water.

On that day all the hearts will become visible — read the *ayat* 'all the secrets will be revealed'.

Just as the three kingdoms are manifest from the power of the elements in his world,

so in the world of the spirit your disposition will either manifest as lights or as fires.

Your behavior and morality will have a new body and a new identity according to that special world.

The distinctions of existence will be removed and neither height nor depth will be recognizable.

The death of the body will not remain in the house of life. The external form and inner spirit will become as one.

Your foot, head, and eye will become as a heart and will become purified of the darkness of your solid form.

The light of the Real will radiate in you and you will clearly see the Real, the Sublime.

You will overturn the order of the worlds — I do not know just how intoxicated you will become.

Reflect on the meaning of 'their Lord gave them to

11th Question to Shabistari

drink' — what is this purified drink other than purification of the self?

What a drink, what a perfume, what sweet taste! What good fortune, what bewilderment, what passion!

It is a happy moment when we are left without the self — then we become infinitely rich and yet utterly in need.

Without the *din* or the intellect, without fear of Allah or perception we would fall drunk and confused into the dust.

What meaning do the Garden, the houris or the servants have here, for no one who is a stranger will bear this intimacy.

As with every intoxication there is painful stupor — my heart is drowned in blood at this thought.

12th Question to Shabistari

How is it that the before-time and the in-time are separate, the one becoming the world and the other God?

The Answer

Before-time and in-time are not separate from each other; the first is temporal, existing by the Eternal-Real.

Everything is Him and this world is a mere fable — except for the Real, names and words have no corresponding things which answer to them.

It is impossible for non-existence to have existence, but

true existence never ends.

Neither is it a question of one thing becoming another or vice versa. All difficulties have now been solved for you.

The cosmos itself is a totally illusionary matter — it is like a point which appears as a circle when it is whirled around.

Go and whirl round a glowing coal, you will see a circle in the rapid movement.

Even if the number one is used in counting, it clearly does not become many by this counting.

Abandon the *hadith* 'what is other than Allah' — use your intellect to distinguish between one thing and the other.

How can you doubt that this is illusion, for duality along with oneness is a total impossibility?

Non-existence, like existence, is single — all plurality becomes manifest in the relative world of phenomena.

The appearance of differences, plurality and activity issues from the chameleon-like world of the phenomenal-possible.

As the existence in everything is one and the same, everything testifies to the oneness of the Real.

13th Question to Shabistari

What does the man of inner understanding mean by those expressions which indicate the eye and the lip? What kind of person is the man of such stations and states?

The Answer

Everything which is visible in this world is like a reflection from the Sun of that world.

The world is like a curl, the down, a mole and the brow — everything being beautiful and each perfectly in its place.

The *tajalli* radiance is sometimes beautiful and sometimes majestic — the face and the curl are metaphors for these meanings.

Subtlety and conquering might are qualities of the Real, the Sublime — the face and curl of fair ones are types of these two.

Since on hearing these words we perceive them through the senses, the immediate result of this is an awareness of objects.

The world of meanings has no boundaries — how can the ordinary eye perceive this?

How can words be found to contain the meanings which are revealed in spiritual tasting?

When the people of hearts explain these meanings they use metaphor to interpret them.

Matter which is perceived by the senses is as a shadow of that world — this world is as the child and that like the mole.

I say that words themselves refer to the meanings of the original state of things.

People have made a habit of applying them to individual objects — what do the common people know about their true meaning?

When the intellect perceived the world, it transferred words from their original meanings.

The man of intellect respects the importance of analogy when he dwells upon the relationship of word and meaning.

The perfect analogy, however, is not possible, but strive

continually to find it.

Nobody can judge you in this matter, for there is no leader of this way other than the Real.

Beware, beware for as long as you have yourself, maintain what is indicated in the *shari'ah*.

The people of hearts have special license in three states — that is, in annihilation, intoxication, and flirtation with the Beloved.

Anyone who experiences these three states knows the use of these words and their meanings.

If you do not experience these states, do not become one who covers up the Real by ignorant imitation of the men of the outer.

The states of reality are not illusory, but not every man understands the secrets of the path.

Oh friend, idle talk does not come from the people of realities — true understanding comes either from an unveiling or from firm belief.

I have explained to you in brief the application of the worlds and their meanings, so if you wish you may understand.

Reflect upon the meanings keeping the end in mind, and be aware of everything which is associated with each meaning.

Demonstrate the meanings from one angle with comparisons, but from another explain them by negating all comparison.

Now that this rule is well established, I will demonstrate it by using several other metaphors.

An Illustration through Metaphor

Look into the eye of the Beloved and see what appears — be aware of what accompanies such perception.

His eye awakens or causes intoxication — the source of existence is revealed from His scarlet red lips.

The hearts become drunk from His eye — all the spirits are veiled by His scarlet lips.

All the hearts are burning because of His eye — His red lips are healing for the sick spirit.

Although the world does not enter His eye, His lip is constantly showing mercy.

He fills the hearts with humanity in a breath, and gives help to the helpless in a breath.

Every glance from Him is as a baited snare — He turns every corner into a wine tavern.

He raises creation to the ground with a glance — He restores it again with a kiss.

Our blood boils hot because of His eye and our spirit is in constant confusion from His lips.

His eye steals the heart with a frown — he cheers the spirit by a smile on His lips.

When you seek intimacy with the eye and lip, one says

yes and the other no.

He finishes the affair of the world with a frown — He is constantly reviving the soul.

We surrender our lives with just a kiss from Him and we are raised up again with just one kiss from Him.

The day of gathering arrives 'in the blink of an eye', and Adam was created with the blowing of the trumpet.

When the world reflects on His eye and His lip, it gives itself up to the worship of wine.

Our whole existence is intoxication or sleep. What connection is there between dust and the Lord of the Lords?

For this reason there are a hundred difficulties in understanding why He said, 'and indeed you were created exactly as I'.

An Illustration through Mithal

The matter of the Beloved's curl is very long. What should be said about this, as it is a question of inner secrets?

Do not question me about the wavy curl — do not shake the chain which makes the mad lovers prisoners!

Last night I spoke clearly about exaltedness but the tip of the curl told me to conceal it.

Thus crookedness overcame straightness and the path of the seeker became tortuous.

All the hearts became enchained by this curl and all the spirits burn with passion.

Hundreds of thousands of hearts are bound from every side: not one heart lies outside of this circle.

If He shook aside his curls, not a single *kafir* would be left in the world.

If He left them always in their place, not a single *mu'min* would remain in the world.

His curl of hair is like a treacherous trap, playfully He undoes the curls from His head.

There would be no cause for sadness if His curls were cut — if the night becomes shorter the length of day increases.

He plunders the caravan of the intellect and imprisons it in knots by His own hand.

His curls are never for a moment at rest — sometimes they bring morning and sometimes night.

He makes a hundred days and nights by His face and His curls — he is constantly making incredible flirtations.

The clay of Adam was intoxicated the moment it was given the sweet scent of the curl.

The heart has a clear understanding of His curl as it too never remains at rest for a moment.

Thus we are being everything afresh in every moment clinging to our hearts within our bodies.

The heart becomes agitated by those curls — the heart becomes inflamed at the sight of His face.

An illustration through Mithal

The cheek is the manifestation of God's beauty — majestic Lordship is meant by the fine down on the skin.

His cheek inscribed a line which encompasses beauty indicating 'there is no beautiful face other than Mine'.

The down is the fertile green of the unseen world — thus it is called the water of life.

See day and night in the blackness of His curl. Seek the spring of life in His down.

Drink like Khidr in his hidden station — His down is the water of life.

If you perceive His down with the eye of certainty you will know how to distinguish multiplicity in oneness.

You understand the matters of this world from the curl and you see clearly the hidden secrets from His down.

Although one man sees the down on his fine face, my heart sees His face in His down.

His face is the seven *ayats* of the opening *surah*. Every letter contains an ocean of meaning.

Hidden beneath each hair on His cheek are thousands of oceans of knowledge from the world of the unseen.

See — your heart is the Throne of the Merciful on the water — from His down comes the beauty of the spirits.

An Illustration through Mithal

The point of the mole on that face is expansive — it encompasses both the center and the circumference.

From it the sphere of the two worlds is drawn and from it is delineated the self and the heart of Adam.

The heart is wounded and bleeding because of that mole for it is the inner reflection of the point of the black mole.

The state of the heart is bleeding blood — there is no escape from this station because of the mole.

Multiplicity has no place in unity — there cannot be two points in the root of unity.

I do not know if His mole is the reflection of our heart or our heart the reflection of the mole on that fair face.

Does the heart become manifest by the reflection of His mole — does the reflection of my heart become visible in that place?

Whether the heart is in His face or He is in the heart, the meaning of this difficult matter is veiled from me.

If this heart of ours is the reflection of that mole, why are there so many different states?

Sometimes it is veiled like His intoxicating eye — sometimes it is trembling like His curl.

Sometimes it is as bright as His moon-like face, sometimes it is dark like the black mole.

Sometimes it is a mosque and sometimes a synagogue,

sometimes the Fire and sometimes the Garden.

Sometimes it is raised above the seventh heaven, sometime it falls lower than this mass of earth.

After doing-without and obedience it again seeks the wine, the lamp and the Beloved.

14th Question to Shabistari

What is the meaning of wine, lamp, and the beautiful Beloved? What is claimed by those whose path is ruin and abandonment?

The Answer

Wine, lamp, and the Beloved are sources of pure meanings — in every outer form these meanings are manifest.

Wine and candle and tasting and the light of gnosis — look at the Beloved who is hidden from no one.

Here the wine is the glass, and the candle the lamp, and the beautiful Beloved the rays of light emanating from the spirits.

Musa's heart scintillated because of the beauty of the Beloved — his wine was the fire and his torch the bush.

The wine and lamp and the beautiful Beloved are all present, so do not forget to play sweetly with the Beloved.

The wine and the lamp are the spirit and lights of the inner journey — witnessing the Beloved means the greatest of His signs.

Kill the self a while with the wine of annihilation — it may be you will find safety and peace from yourself.

Drink the wine until you are rid of yourself and the existence of the drop becomes merged with the ocean.

Drink the wine, for its cup is the face of the Beloved — the cup is His eye drunken with wine.

Seek the wine without cup or goblet — wine is wine drinker, cupbearer is wine cup.

Drink wine from the cup of the Face that goes-on, 'their Lord gave them to drink'. He is the true wine-pourer.

Pure wine is the wine which purifies you of the stain of existence at the time of intoxication.

Drink wine and free yourself from existence, for a bad drunkard is better than one who worships his self.

For someone who is far from the court of the Real, the veil of darkness is better for him than light.

Adam found great relief in darkness and *Iblis* was forever cursed by the light.

Even if the heart's mirror is polished, what good is it if

you only see yourself in it?

Whenever rays of light from His face fall in the wine, many forms bubble up in it.

The world and spirit have the form of the bubbles — for the *awliya* these bubbles are veils.

The intellect which fills the world is confused and dazed at this, and the *nafs* of mankind becomes imprisoned by it.

The whole world is as His wine house, the heart of every atom is His goblet.

Reason is drunk, angels drunk, the spirit drunk, the air drunk, earth drunk, and sky drunk.

The heavens, drunk with wine, move in agitation desiring in their heart to smell His scent.

The angels drink pure wine from pure jugs and pour the remains of their drink onto this earth.

The elements become tipsy with this single draught, sometimes falling into water, sometimes into fire.

From the scent of the draught which falls on the Earth, man goes up until he reaches the heavens.

From its reflection the withered body becomes a living spirit, from its shining rays the dejected spirit flows freely again.

The world of creation is constantly intoxicated by it, always leaving behind its material home.

One man's intellect is awakened by the scent of its dregs. Another becomes forgetful at the sight of its pure color.

Another swallows down in one gulp the cup, the tavern,

the wine-pourer and the wine drinker.

One becomes true in action and word with half a draught, one becomes a lover with just one cupful.

He drinks and drinks and his mouth remains open — what an ocean is the heart, how sublime the reveler.

He drinks up existence in one draught and becomes free of affirmation and negation.

He becomes free of harshness in his doing-without and free of uncontained acts of worship — he clings to the robe of the gnostic *shaykh* in his wine house of annihilation.

The Stations of the Tavern of Annihilation

To become a wasted drunkard is to be freed of the self. The self is *kufr* if it is worshipped.

The people of the tavern of annihilation give indications that *tawhid* is the falling away of the world of phenomena.

The tavern of annihilation is from the world beyond recognizable forms — it is the station of the lovers who no longer care.

The tavern of annihilation is the nest of the bird of the spirit — the tavern of ruin is the threshold of the space beyond place.

The wasted drunkard is ruined in this place of annihilation — from this empty waste the world is as a mirage.

14th Question to Shabistari

The tavern of the self's ruin has no limit, no end — no one has seen its beginning and no one its end.

If you hurry round in it for a hundred years you will neither find your self again nor anyone else.

The group who live there are physically unrecognizable, they are all neither *mu'min* nor *kafir*.

The wine of annihilation of the self has affected their heads — they have abandoned all notion of good actions and wrong actions.

Each has drunk the wine heedless of how much, unaware of its taste — each has done with the feelings of dishonor or fame.

There is talk of what happens with inner expansion and overflow — illusions of *khalwa* and the light of divine gifts,

have all been given up through smelling these dregs — by tasting annihilation they have all fallen drunk in Him.

Staff and bowl, *tasbih* and *miswak* have all been ransomed off for the dregs of wine.

They fall back and then rise again from the water and clay, shedding blood from their eyes instead of tears.

Through intoxication they sometimes rise to the world of ecstasy, holding their necks high like racers.

Sometimes they face the veiling wall of phenomena, black-faced, sometimes facing execution, red flushed with love.

Sometimes in the *sama'* dance of passion for the Beloved they lose all notion of top and bottom and revolve like heavens.

Rapture comes to them from the unseen world with every melody they hear from the singer.

The *sama'* of the spirit is not just sound and words for in every note there is a wonderful secret.

They draw off the folds of their cloak and are stripped of every color and smell.

They drink one cup of the pure wine and become *Sufis*, purified of the qualities of other-than-Him.

They wash away all color — black, green, and blue — in that pure mature wine, and sweep clean the rubbish heap of existence with their eyelashes, not telling the hundredth part of what they see.

They grasp the cloak of the drunken revelers, tired of talk of the *Shaykh* and the *murid*.

What is a *Shaykh* and what is a *murid*, what restrictions are there? What place is there now for doing-without and fear of Allah, what hypocrisy is this?

If your vision is still bounded by quality and quantity, idols and priestly belts and Christianity are better for you.

15th Question to Shabistari

Idols and priestly belts are all *kufr* in this matter of ours.
If this is not so, then say what they are?

The Answer

Here the idol is the outer manifestation of passion and unity. The priestly belt indicates the taking on of the transaction of obedience.

Since both *kufr* and *din* are sustained by His existence, *tawhid* itself becomes an idol worshipped as 'other'.

As everything is a manifestation of His existence every single thing is, in a way, an idol.

Reflect well upon this, oh man of intellect — even the idol is not invalid, given that it exists by Him.

Realize that Allah, the Sublime, is the Creator of it, and from the Good only good becomes manifest.

Existence, wherever it is, is absolutely perfect — if there appears to be any bad in it, then it is from other-than-Allah.

If the muslim understood what the idols were he would recognize with certainty that *din* may also be an object of worship.

If the *mushrik* became aware of what the idols were, how could he go wrong in his *din*?

For him the only idols are visible objects and it is for this reason that he is *kafir* according to the *shari'ah*.

If you see the Real hidden in the idol, then you too are not counted as a muslim according to the *shari'ah*.

The man to whom true *kufr* has been made plain becomes disgusted with an Islam of mere appearance.

A hidden spirit lies within every idol and *iman* lies within *kufr*.

Kufr is in constant praise of the Real — the *ayat* 'all things praise Him' says this; who can deny it?

What should I say — I have strayed far from the Path; 'leave them, and when the message has been delivered say, Allah'.

Who adorned the form of the idol with such beauty? Who could become an idol-worshipper if the Real did not will it?

It is He that acts, He that speaks and He that exists — His action is good, His speech is good and He is good.

See one thing, say one and know one! The root and branches of *iman* are contained in this.

It is not I who say this. Listen to it from the Qur'an: 'There is no split in the creation of the Merciful'.

I have looked and examined the root of everything — the belt worn by the Christians is an indication of obedience.

The people of knowledge do not trust anything unless they see its source.

Bind in your belt like a real man — join the company who fulfill my transaction.

Take control of the ball of happiness from the field by using the horse of knowledge and the stick of worship.

He only created you for this purpose, although He created many creatures besides you.

As knowledge is the father, and the mother action, the different stations of inwardness are 'coolness to the eye'.

There is no doubt that no man is without a father. There is not more than one prophet 'Isa.

Leave tales of wild inner travel and spiritual overwhelming — leave illusions of light and striving for miracles.

In this matter your miracles are only in worship of the Real — anything else is pride, vanity, wonder and illusion.

In this path anything other than poverty is only a cause

for vain ambition and deception.

Breaking the norms of reality have occurred a thousand times at the hand of cursed *Iblis*, who does not witness Reality.

Sometimes he appears through walls, sometimes through the roof. Sometimes he sits in the heart and sometimes the body.

He knows all the hidden stations and causes *kufr*, corruption and rebellion in you.

Your *Iblis* becomes your spiritual leader and you the follower — when will you be capable of all these things?

Miracles are merely examples of exhibiting one's self — you become pharaoh and make divine claims.

Anyone who is truly intimate with Allah never vaunts himself.

Take heed that your gaze is not always on creation — do not allow yourself to be trapped in this way.

If you keep company with the common people you become like them.

Be careful to have no dealings with the common, lest your natural balance be suddenly overturned.

You have wasted your precious life in idle talk. Do you not reflect upon what sort of life you are leading?

The common call their life 'society', but in fact it is confusion. They have a donkey as leader but what a beard he has!

Leadership has degenerated into ignorance, and because

15th Question to Shabistari

of this the people are in a bad state.

Look at the one-eyed Dajjal and how he has been sent into the world as an example.

Examine this example oh man of discrimination; the man who is the ass, is called Jassas.

When the Lord related what would happen at the end of time, he explained the meaning of this on several occasions.

Look now how the leaders have become blind and unaware — all knowledge of the *din* has gone to heaven.

Modestly and courtesy no longer remain with them. No one is ashamed of his ignorance.

The whole order of the world has been turned upside down. If you are a man of reflection look what state it is in.

The man who was criticized, cursed and hated before is now a *shaykh* of the age because his father was good.

Khidr killed that bad son because his father and grandfather were men of correct action.

How you have made an ass of yourself by having a *shaykh* who is more an ass than yourself.

As he does not know the well from the sick, how can he purify your secret?

If the son shows a trace of his father, what should I say but that he is light upon light?

The son who is good in action and of a fortunate disposition is like the ripe fruit at the top of the tree.

But how can he be a *shaykh* of the *din* who does not

know good from evil, bad from good?

To be a *murid* is to learn knowledge of the *din* and to light up the lamp of the heart with light.

Nobody has ever learned knowledge from a dead man. A lamp has never been lit by mere ashes.

Everything indicates to my heart that I should bind on my belt in readiness for this business.

Not in the sense that I may gain fame — this I have, but I am ashamed of it.

My fellow *shaykhs* have shown themselves base in this matter — my obscurity is better than their fame.

Inspiration came to me again from the Real — do not complain about wisdom if in the hands of a fool.

If there were no scavengers in the world, the whole kingdom would be in a mess.

The species of man links everything together — the world is like this and Allah knows best.

Avoid the company of those not on the path — if you wish to serve them break norms.

Slavery and rigid custom do not go together, so be a slave and abandon norms.

Concerning Christianity

I see the aim of Christianity as stripping away of self and becoming free of mechanically following the *shari'ah*.

15th Question to Shabistari

The Lord, Who is Pure and Who is One, is the retreat of the spirit, and the retreat is the nest of the bird-king who lives on after death.

Ruhullah (*'Isa*) made this matter manifest in his life — the teaching was brought to him by the pure spirit of Jibril.

Your spirit is also from Allah and in it is an indication of the pure spirit.

If you become purified of the lower self you may find the presence of the divine, pure Lord.

Anyone who has stripped away the self becomes like an angel and will rise like 'Isa, Spirit of Allah, to the fourth heaven.

The sucking baby is closely confined to this mother and to the cradle.

When he reaches maturity and becomes a man of travel, he goes the way of his father (of meaning) if he is truly a man.

The elements of the Earth are as the maternal mother for you — you are the son and your father is the celestial father of sublimity.

That is why 'Isa when returning to his Lord said, 'I am journeying to my father of meaning who is above'.

You too who are the spirit of your father of meaning journey towards the father! Your fellow travellers in the path have gone, so you go too.

If you want to become a flying bird, throw the carrion world to the vultures.

Give the treacherous world to the common, as carrion should only be given to dogs.

What importance do family relationships have? Seek a fitting relation with the Real and abandon personal relations.

Anyone plunging in the sea of before-creation has Allah's warning, 'personal relations are of no use,' as his currency.

Every relationship which is based on lust leads only to pride and arrogance.

If lust were not involved, relationship would appear unreal, like a dream.

When sexual passion is the active force, one person becomes the mother and the other the father.

I am not saying who the mother and father are, for you should live courteously with them.

The deficient in sense is called a sister, the envious is called a brother.

Your own enemy may be called the son and anyone a stranger to you, your own people.

Tell me what is the nature of the paternal and maternal uncle? Nothing comes from them but pain and sorrow.

Oh brother, the companions who are with you on the path are also companions in frivolity.

If you sit for a while on their paths of good fortune, what good can you say you see of them?

All are unreal and constrictions for you — by the spirit

of the Prophet they are nothing but delusion.

Abandon yourself like a true man, but do not violate the rights of anyone else.

If even the smallest detail of the *shari'ah* is disregarded, you will be outside the parameters of the *din* in both worlds.

Beware lest you do not fulfill the laws of the *shari'ah,* but also at the same time take care of yourself.

Nothing but a store of pain comes from gold and women. Abandon them as 'Isa abandoned Maryam.

Become a *hanif*, without the restriction of any particular *madhhab* — enter a Christian retreat like a monk.

As long as you see other-than-Allah in creation, even being in a mosque is exactly the same as a Christian retreat.

When the veil of otherness disappears before you the mosque becomes just as a Christian retreat for you.

I do not know where you have reached on the path, but oppose the *kafir* self.

Idols, belts, Christianity and bells all indicate the giving up of fame and name.

If you want to become a special servant, prepare yourself to be true and pure in action and thought.

Go and extricate the self from its own pattern and seize hold of *iman* again with every moment.

As long as there is a *kafir* in our inward self, do not be satisfied with an Islam of outward appearances.

Fresh *iman* will flow from you at every moment. Be a muslim! Be a muslim! Be a muslim!

Indeed *iman* is born of *kufr* but in reality it is not *kufr* from which *iman* is increased.

Abandon action due to be seen — abandon fame — throw off the cloak and bind on the Christian belt.

Become as a *Shaykh* of Instruction — devote your heart to manliness if you are a man.

Strip away all affirmation and negation and surrender your heart to the purest Christian — 'Isa.

By what light are the Christian idols manifest that radiance appears on the faces of the idols?

They attract all the hearts with passion — now it is the minstrel, now the wine-pourer.

What a minstrel! He sets on fire the accretions of the self of a hundred spiritual travellers with one sweet tune.

What a wine-pourer! He delivers two hundred men of seventy years from their selves with a single cup.

When he enters the *khanqah* of His remembrance drunken at night, he makes marvelous stories about *Sufis* even more incredible.

And if he enters the mosque at early dawn, he does not leave one man sober.

When he enters the school unrecognized in a drunken state, the *faqih* teacher becomes hopelessly drunk.

The people of doing-without become hopelessly in love with him, and become outcasts from house and home.

He makes one man a *mu'min*, one a *kafir* — he fills the whole world with calamity and wrong.

Taverns of annihilation of the self have been built by his lips — mosques are filled with light by his face.

This business of mine has become easy through him — I have become freed of my *kafir* self.

My heart was prevented through pride from knowing itself and through conceit, vanity, deception, and illusion.

This idol came in at my door before dawn and awakened me from the sleep of forgetfulness.

My hidden spirit was illuminated by his face and by him I saw who I was.

When I looked at his beautiful face my spirit gave a sign of wonder.

He said to me, 'Oh hypocrite? You have spent your life seeking name and fame.'

Look and see what this knowledge, pride doing without and illusion are; you who have not arrived, what kept you back?

To look into one's face for a moment is worth a thousand years of obedience.

In short, the face of that world adorner was shown to me and unveiled in that very instant.

The face of my spirit became black with shame, because of my past life and useless days.

But when that moon whose face is as the Sun saw that I had cut off hope from my spirit.

He filled up a goblet and gave it to me and its liquid lit up a fire in me.

He then said, 'Wash off the forms on the tablet of existence with this colorless wine.'

When I had drunk the goblet to the last drop, I fell down drunk into the dust.

Now I neither exist in myself nor do I exist at all — I am neither awake, intoxicated, nor drunk.

Sometimes I am happy like His eye — sometimes I am confused like His curls.

Sometimes I exist in a place of dirt and ashes because of the nature of myself, sometimes I find myself in a garden of flowers.

I have taken this secret from that garden and have given it the name 'the secret garden'.

In it the flowers of the heart's secrets are blooming — secrets which have never been told before.

The tongues of the lilies are all speaking — the eyes of the narcissus are all looking.

Reflect upon each with the eye of the heart, so that all doubts vanish from you.

Examine the knowledge's arrived at by intellect and the knowledge's of Islamic tradition — examine them in a clear order and with precision.

Do not look with the eye of negation and criticism, for then the flowers will turn to thorns before your eyes.

Ingratitude is a sign of ignorance; knowledge of truth is recognition and gratitude.

I hope when the noble remembers me he will pray

'mercy be upon him'.

I am finishing and sealing this with my own name. Oh Allah, give me the station of Mahmud, the praised One.

www.ingramcontent.com/pod-product-compliance
Lightning Source LLC
Chambersburg PA
CBHW060201050426
42446CB00013B/2931